THIS BOOK
BELONGS TO

____

____

____

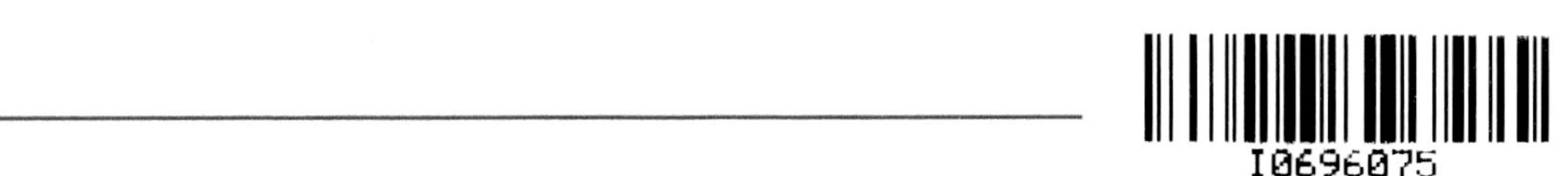

Vicky Rasinske

No protion of this book may be reproduced in whole or in part shared with others, stored in a retriveal system,digitized or transmitted in any from without written persission from the author.

COLOR TEST

Basic tips of Drawing!

- ★ A little bit of art theory is always good to know, Lets start........

- ★ All you need is a pencil,eraser and a piece off paper!

- ★ Draw lightly at first because you might need to erase some lines as you work.

- ★ Add details according to the diagrams but dont worry about being perfect. Artists frequently make mistakes they just find ways to make their mistakes look interesting.

- ★ Dont worry if your drawing dont turn out the way you want them to , just keep practicing ! Sometimes drawing the same thing just a few times will help.

- ★ Once you have finished your drawing in pencil you can trace it with a black fineliner pen and color or paint it to your liking.

Turn the page for some cool composition ideas!!!

COLORING BOOK
THANKS FOR YOUR SUPPORT

THANKS
for the
LOVE

THANK
YOU!

www.ingramcontent.com/pod-product-compliance
Lightning Source LLC
Chambersburg PA
CBHW081225250726

48659CB00018B/2635